God Made Us & Loves Us

Unveiling the Truth:

Faith, Love, and the LGBTQ+ Journey Through Scripture and History

Table of Contents

Anthony P. Brown

Copyright Notice

Cover Art & Design

Ogundiran Olawunmi

Email: ajandell@yahoo.com

Photographer

Anthony P. Brown

Legal Disclaimer

The content of *God Made Us and Loves Us!* is intended for informational, educational, and spiritual exploration. This book seeks to provide historical, theological, and scholarly perspectives on LGBTQ+ identities in relation to religious faith, particularly within Christianity. While extensive research has been conducted to ensure accuracy, interpretations of biblical texts and historical records may vary. Readers are encouraged to engage in their own study and consult religious leaders, theologians, and historians for further insight.

This book does not claim to speak on behalf of any religious institution, denomination, or governing body. The theological perspectives, scriptural analysis, and historical accounts presented are meant to offer alternative viewpoints that challenge traditional interpretations. The intent is not to discredit any individual's faith, beliefs, or religious convictions but rather to foster understanding, inclusivity, and open dialogue.

The historical and scientific discussions within this book are based on available research and scholarly interpretations. However, the fields of theology, history, and science are ever-evolving, and new discoveries or interpretations may emerge over time. This book does not claim to provide absolute truth but rather to encourage critical thinking and deeper exploration.

The author and publisher assume no responsibility for how readers interpret or apply the information presented. *God Made Us and Loves Us!* should not be used as a substitute for professional theological, historical, psychological, or legal advice. Any actions taken based on the content of this book are the sole responsibility of the reader.

All Bible verses cited are from publicly available translations, including the King James Version (KJV) and the New International Version (NIV). Quotations from these translations are used for educational and analytical purposes.

By reading this book, you acknowledge that its contents are presented as an exploration of faith and identity and that religious interpretation is deeply personal and subjective. This book is meant to inspire dialogue, healing, and self-acceptance for those who have been marginalized or excluded due to their sexual orientation or gender identity.

Adrian D. Thompson, Sr.

Dedication & Inspiration

In loving memory of **Sarah "Jo" Julia Inez Herndon-Brown**. (December 7, 1934-November 3, 1995) my dearly beloved mother for her unconditional love and support. One who loved me in spite of, no matter what, and just because. For always being there for me and being my biggest cheerleader. I thank you for teaching me the real meaning of faith and believing in self. I remember a profound quote you would always say to me, "Whatever you become in life, be the very best". Lastly, thank you for being my very best friend and most of all teaching me the power of prayer.

Robert D. Miller, Jr. The world's greatest Uncle/Dad. Thank you for being the only real father figure I ever had in my life. Thank you for always believing in me no matter what. Even when I didn't always believe in myself. You taught me how to have courage to be able to face adversities in life, always having my back, showing up when I was at my lowest. Thank you for just being there when I needed you the most. Thank you for also being my friend.

Joshua D. Brown, my nephew. The day you passed away, a part of me went with you. Although there are other nephews and nieces, there was something special about you. It is not a day that goes by that you are not in my thoughts. I feel God placed you here on earth temporarily or just for a season to impart into my life, which you did in so many ways. Thank you for teaching me forgiveness. You will always be my "little buggah". (As tears flow from my eyes).

A. **Lynn Harris, J. L. King, James Earl Hardy, Craig Stewart, Will Horn** and **Steven T. Smith**, all Black authors, you all have been inspirational in my work as a writer. You all created the blueprint to show the world and other people of color that this can be done and how to share our thoughts with the world. I thank each of you for running the race and not giving up on your dreams.

Dedication:

To all of the boys and girls who wonder if God loves you?

To the parents who are struggling with how to love your queer child?

To the religious leaders losing some of your flock to the world.

It is my prayer that after reading this book you will find your answers.

Foreword

For centuries, LGBTQ+ individuals have faced exclusion, judgment, and condemnation from religious institutions that claim to speak on behalf of God. Many have struggled with their faith, torn between their love for God and the overwhelming belief that their very existence is sinful. The pain of this conflict has led to untold suffering—families divided, souls burdened, and countless individuals feeling as if they must choose between their faith and their identity.

But what if that choice was never meant to exist? What if the rejection so many have experienced is not from God, but from flawed human interpretations?

God Made Us and Loves Us! is a book that challenges centuries of harmful doctrine and unveils a truth that has been buried under layers of misinterpretation, cultural bias, and institutionalized discrimination. It is a book of love, acceptance, and affirmation—one that seeks to bridge the gap between faith and identity, proving that they were never meant to be at odds in the first place.

As you turn these pages, you will embark on a journey through scripture, history, and science. You will discover that the Bible does not actually condemn same-sex relationships in the way many have been led to believe. Through careful analysis of biblical texts, this book reveals how mistranslations, cultural context, and human influence have shaped modern religious beliefs about sexuality. You will read about same-sex love within the Bible itself—stories of deep devotion, spiritual connection, and unwavering loyalty that have been overlooked or deliberately erased.

Beyond scripture, *God Made Us and Loves Us!* delves into history, showing that same-sex love has always existed across cultures and civilizations. Long before modern religious doctrine imposed rigid definitions of love and gender, societies around the world honored and accepted LGBTQ+ individuals. The book exposes how the shift toward condemnation was not rooted in divine truth, but in human ambition and political maneuvering within the Christian church.

Science, too, affirms what history and scripture already tell us—that same-sex attraction is natural, normal, and deeply ingrained in the fabric of life itself.

From the animal kingdom to the study of human genetics, *God Made Us and Loves Us!* presents undeniable evidence that being LGBTQ+ is not an anomaly, but a beautiful part of creation.

This book is more than an academic study; it is a lifeline. It is for the believer who has spent years in silent turmoil, wondering if God still loves them. It is for the parent struggling to reconcile their faith with their child's identity. It is for the pastors and religious leaders seeking to create a more inclusive and loving church community. It is for anyone who has ever questioned the idea that God's love is conditional.

God Made Us and Loves Us! is a message of hope, a call for understanding, and an invitation to see the divine in all people. The truth is simple yet profound: God made you exactly as you are. And He loves you—fully, unconditionally, and without exception.

May this book bring you the peace, clarity, and affirmation you deserve.

— **Jabari Philmore**

Foreword

As a lifelong believer, I have always held onto the truth that God is love. Yet, throughout history, that love has often been distorted, confined, and weaponized to exclude those who do not fit into rigid, man-made doctrines. Nowhere is this more evident than in the treatment of LGBTQ+ individuals within religious spaces.

For too long, faith and identity have been pitted against each other, forcing many to feel like they must choose between the God they love and the truth of who they are. This has led to generations of unnecessary suffering—people cast out of their homes, churches, and communities, all because of a narrative built on misinterpretation and prejudice rather than divine truth.

That is why God Made Us and Loves Us! is such an essential book. It stands as both a testament and a challenge—a testament to the unwavering love of God for all His children and a challenge to the traditions that have sought to limit the vastness of that love.

This book is more than just an exploration of scripture; it is a call to unlearn and relearn, to re-examine the Bible in its historical and cultural context, and to confront the ways in which mistranslations and bias have shaped the modern understanding of same-sex relationships. Through detailed biblical analysis, this book lays bare the reality that many of the passages used to condemn LGBTQ+ individuals have been taken out of context or altered through centuries of linguistic evolution. It highlights the truth that the Bible, at its core, is a story of love, faith, and justice—not exclusion and condemnation.

But this book does not stop at scripture alone. It also turns to history, demonstrating that same-sex love is not a modern concept but an integral part of human existence across all cultures and time periods. Long before religious institutions imposed their restrictive views, civilizations around the world celebrated and honored diverse expressions of love and identity. By weaving together theological insight, historical evidence, and scientific affirmation, this book serves as an undeniable testament that LGBTQ+ people have always been, and will always be, a natural and divine part of creation.

Perhaps most importantly, this book serves as a source of healing. It speaks to those who have been made to feel unworthy, sinful, or broken simply because of who they love.

It reassures parents seeking guidance, pastors striving for inclusivity, and believers who yearn for a faith that embraces rather than excludes. It provides hope for those who have been cast aside by their religious communities, affirming that their faith is still valid, their love is still holy, and their existence is still a reflection of God's infinite and perfect design.

God Made Us and Loves Us! is not just a book—it is a movement, a revelation, and a bridge for those who have been led to believe that God's love has limits.

This book dares to say what should have always been known: that love, in all its forms, is divine. And that every single person, regardless of who they love, is cherished, accepted, and wholly embraced by the Creator.

To those who read these pages, may you find the affirmation you seek, the answers you need, and the love you deserve. Because the truth remains unshaken: God made you, and He loves you—without condition, without exception, and without end.

— Apostle Dr. Donallen Lowe

The Impact Center Dallas, TX & FL

Synopsis: "God Made Us and Loves Us!"

For too long, LGBTQ+ individuals have been told that their existence contradicts their faith. Many have been pushed to believe that the Bible condemns same-sex relationships, leading to pain, isolation, and inner conflict. But what if the truth has been distorted? What if scripture, history, and nature itself prove that same-sex love has always been part of God's creation?

"God Made Us and Loves Us!" is a powerful exploration of faith, history, and love. This book dismantles centuries of misinterpretation, revealing how biblical passages often used to condemn LGBTQ+ people have been mistranslated or taken out of context. It shines a light on same-sex love within the Bible itself, presenting stories of deep devotion and spiritual connection that have been overlooked for generations.

Beyond scripture, this book dives into history, proving that same-sex love has existed since the dawn of civilization. From ancient Mesopotamia to Indigenous cultures across the globe, societies have honored and accepted LGBTQ+ identities long before modern religious doctrine imposed restrictions. It exposes how anti-LGBTQ+ beliefs were not born from divine will but from cultural and political forces that shaped Christianity over time.

With scientific evidence supporting the natural existence of same-sex attraction, testimonies from LGBTQ+ Christians who have reconciled their faith and identity, and a vision for a more inclusive future, *"God Made Us and Loves Us!"* is a beacon of hope. It is a resource for parents seeking to understand their queer children, for believers struggling with their identity, and for anyone looking to embrace the truth that God's love knows no bounds.

This book is more than just a study—it is a call for love, acceptance, and spiritual liberation. Because the truth is simple: God made you exactly as you are. And He loves you.

About The Author: Embracing Love and Truth

For centuries, LGBTQ+ individuals have struggled to reconcile their love for God with their true selves. Many have been told that their existence is an abomination, that their love is unnatural, and that their faith and identity cannot coexist. Yet, what if the very scriptures used to condemn same-sex love actually reveal a deeper message of acceptance? What if history itself proves that same-sex love has always been part of the human experience? This book is an exploration of faith, history, and love—a resource for those seeking answers, affirmation, and truth.

I am **Anthony Brown**. I am a believer. I was raised in the church, taught to fear and revere God from an early age. I became an ordained minister, a prayer warrior, sang in the church choir, someone deeply committed to faith and spiritual growth. Yet, my journey has not been without struggle. I have been on both sides of the spectrum—a devout Christian at one point, and an atheist at another. My life has been a constant search for truth, for understanding, for a way to make sense of the contradictions I witnessed in faith communities. I have attended various churches and denominations, seeking answers from different perspectives, longing to understand the fullness of God's truth.

Through this journey, I have experienced both the warmth of church love and the devastating wounds of church hurt. I have seen the hypocrisy of those who preach love yet condemn without understanding. I have felt the sting of rejection from those who claim to follow Christ but refuse to extend His grace to all. And yet, through it all, I never stopped seeking God. Even in my moments of doubt, when I turned away from faith, God never turned away from me.

This book started as a personal research project, a way for me to finally uncover the truth for myself. I wanted to understand what God really says about same-sex love, beyond what had been preached to me. I dug into scripture, studied historical texts, and examined scientific research. The more I learned, the more my heart burned with the realization that everything I had been told about LGBTQ+ condemnation was based on mistranslations, cultural biases, and human interpretation rather than divine truth.

Then, God spoke to me: "I gave you this knowledge for a reason. Now, share it with the world."

This book is the result of that divine instruction. It is my testimony, my offering, my mission to spread the truth that has been hidden for too long. It is a message of hope for those who have been cast out by their families, their churches, and their communities. It is a call for reconciliation for those who have been told they must choose between their faith and their identity. It is an affirmation that God's love is limitless, unconditional, and all-encompassing.

Throughout the pages of this book, we will explore the misinterpretations of scripture that have been used to condemn LGBTQ+ individuals. We will uncover the hidden stories of same-sex love in the Bible. We will look at history to see how societies before Christianity embraced same-sex relationships without shame or judgment. We will examine the ways in which religious institutions have manipulated scripture for power and control. And finally, we will explore the overwhelming scientific and historical evidence that proves LGBTQ+ people are a natural and beautiful part of God's creation.

If you have ever questioned whether God loves you, let me assure you: He does. He made you exactly as you are, in His image, with a purpose and a plan. You do not have to choose between your faith and your identity. You are not an abomination. You are not a mistake. You are fearfully and wonderfully made.

This book is for every LGBTQ+ person who has ever sat in a church pew feeling unworthy. It is for every parent struggling to reconcile their child's identity with their faith. It is for the pastors and religious leaders who want to foster a church that truly embodies Christ's love. It is for anyone who has ever asked the question: Can I be queer and still be loved by God?

The answer is simple: Yes, you can. Because ***God made you, and He loves you.***

— **Anthony P. Brown**, Author

Rum, Lies & The Pastor's Wife

The American Mogul and His Nigerian Kings

State of Desire

1

Understanding

Biblical Context and Interpretation

The Bible and Same-Sex Love – Misunderstood, Mistranslated, and Misused

"You shall know the truth, and the truth shall make you free."

— John 8:32 (NRSV)

For centuries, the Bible has been weaponized against LGBTQ+ people. Verses pulled from ancient texts—often out of context—have been used to justify judgment, exclusion, and even violence. Yet when we peel back the layers of translation history, cultural context, and theological bias, what emerges is not condemnation but complexity—and ultimately, a message of divine love.

Originally written in Hebrew, Aramaic, and Koine Greek, the Bible reflects the cultural and linguistic frameworks of the societies in which it was written. Over time, as translations passed through Latin, German, English, and hundreds of other languages, many words and concepts shifted meaning. These shifts—sometimes subtle, sometimes drastic—have altered how certain passages are understood, especially regarding human sexuality.

In this chapter, we will:

1. Examine commonly misused scriptures.
2. Revisit the historical context in which they were written.
3. Introduce examples of same-sex love and intimacy from biblical times.
4. Explore how faithful LGBTQ+ inclusion is consistent with the Bible's overarching message of love, justice, and mercy.

Part 1: Scripture Under the Microscope – Misinterpretation and Misuse

We've previously analyzed key scriptures often used to condemn same-sex relationships, including Leviticus 18:22, Romans 1:26–27, and 1 Corinthians 6:9–10. Let's now revisit these with new depth and theological clarity.

Leviticus and Ritual Purity

The Holiness Code (Leviticus 17–26) served to set the Israelites apart from neighboring tribes. It was a religious, not civil or moral, document. It forbade shaving the sides of one's beard (Leviticus 19:27), wearing blended fabrics, and eating pork or shrimp—alongside the now-infamous Leviticus 18:22 and 20:13. These laws were meant for a specific people in a specific time.

What most readers don't realize is that ancient same-sex acts were usually performed within religious rituals—temple prostitution, fertility rites, or cultic sacrifices. They were not reflections of orientation or loving unions.

Romans and Roman Decadence

Paul's letter to the Romans is often cited as a blanket condemnation of same-sex acts. But Paul's actual concern was idol worship and unrestrained, excessive lust common in Roman society. This included orgies, pederasty (older men with boys), and coercive sexual practices tied to religious rites. What Paul critiques are power-driven, exploitative relationships—not mutual, consensual love.

Romans 2 continues by condemning the hypocrisy of those who judge others while committing their own injustices, further emphasizing Paul's rhetorical intent.

Arsenokoitai: The Greek Word No One Understands

In both 1 Corinthians 6:9 and 1 Timothy 1:10, the word *arsenokoitai* is used—yet it appears nowhere else in ancient Greek literature. Its exact meaning remains a mystery. Some believe it refers to male prostitution, others to economic exploitation involving sex. But nowhere does it clearly denote "homosexual" as we understand it today.

In fact, "homosexuality" as a concept—an innate, unchangeable orientation—did not even exist until the 19th century. The ancients did not categorize people by sexual orientation but by roles and status. As a result, reading modern understandings into ancient texts creates grave interpretative errors.

Part 2: Historical Evidence of Same-Sex Love in Biblical Times

Despite centuries of silence and suppression, history contains numerous examples of same-sex love, even within the biblical narrative.

1. David and Jonathan – A Love That Surpassed That of Women

> *"Your love to me was wonderful, more than the love of women."*

— 2 Samuel 1:26 (NRSV)

The story of David and Jonathan is one of the most emotionally rich male relationships in the Bible. Jonathan, the son of King Saul, forms an immediate and profound bond with David. The Bible describes how Jonathan "loved David as his own soul" (1 Samuel 18:1), gave him his royal robe and armor (a symbolic act of covenant), and made a sacred pact with him.

Their relationship involved deep emotional intimacy, covenantal language, and physical expression (they kissed and wept together, 1 Samuel 20:41). While some interpret this as platonic, others—including biblical scholars and LGBTQ+ theologians—see it as reflective of romantic or even erotic love.

Biblical scholar Dr. Theodore Jennings Jr. and queer theologian Dr. Mona West argue that the text's language, particularly David's declaration that Jonathan's love was "greater than the love of women," implies a bond beyond friendship.

2. Ruth and Naomi – "Where You Go, I Will Go"

> *"Where you go, I will go; where you lodge, I will lodge; your people shall be my people, and your God my God."*

— Ruth 1:16

Ruth, a Moabite widow, binds herself to her Israelite mother-in-law Naomi with a vow that echoes the language of marriage covenants. The intimacy of their bond, the shared life, the deep emotional attachment—these have led many scholars to explore the possibility of romantic affection.

While Ruth later marries Boaz (to secure lineage), the text centers her emotional loyalty and spiritual kinship with Naomi. Lesbian theologians such as Dr. Virginia Ramey Mollenkott and Rev. Dr. Nancy Wilson consider Ruth and Naomi's story an important example of female solidarity and potentially romantic commitment in scripture.

3. The Centurion and His Beloved Servant

"Lord, my servant lies at home paralyzed, suffering terribly."

— Matthew 8:6

In Matthew 8, a Roman centurion approaches Jesus to heal his *pais*—a Greek word that can mean "servant," "son," or "boy lover." In Roman culture, it was not uncommon for centurions to have male slaves who were also sexual companions. While modern translations often use the word "servant," the original Greek leaves room for broader interpretation.

Jesus does not rebuke the centurion. In fact, he praises his faith and heals the beloved without hesitation.

If the relationship was indeed romantic, Jesus' response is especially significant—he offers healing, not judgment.

Part 3: Cultural Context and Queer Inclusion

Ancient Near East and Greco-Roman Attitudes

In ancient Mesopotamia, Egypt, and Greece, same-sex relationships were often visible—though regulated by class and gender roles. In Sumerian mythology, gods like Enki and Dumuzi had intimate, possibly erotic relationships. Greek philosophers like Plato, Socrates, and Phaedrus openly discussed male love as a noble form of affection and intellectual bond.

In the Roman Empire, sex was about power and status more than gender. Freeborn male citizens could penetrate lower-class men or slaves without social stigma—but to be penetrated, or to show emotional vulnerability,

was seen as weakness. These dynamics are what Paul addresses—not two equals in love, but domination and abuse.

Sexuality in Biblical Languages

Neither Hebrew nor Greek has words equivalent to "homosexual" or "gay." Instead, sexual behavior was described in terms of action, not identity. Thus, modern Bibles that insert "homosexuals" into ancient texts are guilty of *anachronism*—imposing modern categories on ancient contexts.

Part 4: Toward an Inclusive Theology

Jesus summarized the law with two commandments:

1. Love God.
2. Love your neighbor as yourself.

He broke societal taboos, dined with outcasts, and extended grace to those deemed "unclean." He never once mentioned same-sex relationships. If LGBTQ+ people were truly outside of God's plan, wouldn't Jesus—God incarnate—have addressed it directly?

Instead, he offered healing, inclusion, and love to all.

The Fruits of the Spirit and Queer Lives

Galatians 5:22–23 tells us that the fruits of the Spirit are love, joy, peace, patience, kindness, goodness, faithfulness, gentleness, and self-control.

Many LGBTQ+ relationships bear these fruits—often in the face of immense adversity.

By their fruits, you will know them.

Conclusion: Reclaiming the Sacred for All People

It is time to reclaim the Bible from those who use it as a weapon. The scriptures, when read with honesty and reverence, reveal not a message of exclusion—but of radical love.

LGBTQ+ people are not an aberration. We are part of God's design, part of God's family, and part of God's story.

Just as the early church eventually welcomed Gentiles, embraced women as leaders, and challenged the institution of slavery, so too must we grow in our understanding of love and justice.

God made us and loves us. Entirely. Unapologetically. Eternally.

Let this truth set you free.

2

Same-Sex Love

in the Bible

Contrary to popular belief, the Bible contains multiple examples of deep, same-sex love and devotion.

While many modern theologians and church traditions have overlooked or reinterpreted these connections to fit heteronormative ideologies, the original scriptures, when studied in their proper context and with honesty, tell a very different story. Relationships of deep emotional, spiritual, and possibly even romantic intimacy between people of the same sex are not condemned in the Bible—in fact, some are honored, respected, and deeply mourned when broken by death.

This chapter will unpack those narratives through the lens of scripture, drawing from both the **King James Version (KJV)** and **New International Version (NIV)** for balance, and confront the often-suppressed truths about **King James I**, the monarch behind the KJV.

David and Jonathan: A Love Beyond Friendship

Perhaps the most compelling same-sex bond in the Bible is between **David**, who would become king of Israel, and **Jonathan**, the son of King Saul. Their relationship is introduced in **1 Samuel 18**, shortly after David defeats Goliath.

◈ **1 Samuel 18:1 (KJV)**

> *"The soul of Jonathan was knit with the soul of David, and Jonathan loved him as his own soul."*

◈ **1 Samuel 18:1 (NIV)**

> *"Jonathan became one in spirit with David, and he loved him as himself."*

This is not a casual friendship—it's described in covenantal, soul-deep language, similar to the Genesis description of Adam and Eve becoming "one flesh." In verse 3, the Bible says:

◈ **1 Samuel 18:3 (KJV)**

> *"Then Jonathan and David made a covenant, because he loved him as his own soul."*

◈ **1 Samuel 18:3 (NIV)**

> *"And Jonathan made a covenant with David because he loved him as himself."*

This "covenant" is not military or political—it is emotional and personal. It echoes ancient marriage pacts in its structure and language. Jonathan then strips himself of his robe, sword, bow, and belt, and gives them to David. Symbolically, this act represents Jonathan laying down his royal succession rights and armor to David—out of love.

The depth of their relationship is further shown in **1 Samuel 20**, when Jonathan and David must part due to Saul's threats. Their goodbye is filled with raw emotion and physical affection.

◈ **1 Samuel 20:41 (KJV)**

> *"They kissed one another, and wept one with another, until David exceeded."*

◈ **1 Samuel 20:41 (NIV)**

> *"Then they kissed each other and wept together—but David wept the most."*

This act is not a casual goodbye; it's heart-wrenching, intimate, and reflective of a deep, soul-connected love.

When Jonathan is later killed in battle, David mourns him with one of the most passionate elegies recorded in scripture.

◈ **2 Samuel 1:26 (KJV)**

"I am distressed for thee, my brother Jonathan: very pleasant hast thou been unto me: thy love to me was wonderful, passing the love of women."

◈ **2 Samuel 1:26 (NIV)**

"I grieve for you, Jonathan my brother; you were very dear to me. Your love for me was wonderful, more wonderful than that of women."

This verse cannot be overlooked. David, who had multiple wives, compares Jonathan's love favorably to the love he received from women—explicitly saying it surpassed them. Biblical scholars and queer theologians have pointed out that this language, coupled with their covenant and affectionate parting, is consistent with romantic love.

Some traditionalists argue that it was merely a "brotherly love." But nowhere else in the Bible do male friends share this level of covenantal intimacy, physical closeness, and poetic devotion. If Jonathan were a woman, no one would question the romantic nature of this story.

King James I: A Historical Note on the Man Behind the Translation

It is important to examine the life of **King James I of England**, the monarch who authorized the 1611 English translation of the Bible that bears his name. Historical records and personal letters reveal compelling evidence that King James was himself attracted to men and possibly engaged in romantic or sexual relationships with male courtiers.

James had intense, emotionally charged relationships with at least three men, most notably **Robert Carr, Earl of Somerset**, and later **George Villiers, Duke**

of Buckingham. Letters between James and Villiers include language more akin to lovers than statesmen:

> *"I desire only to live in this world for your sake... I had rather live banished in any part of the earth with you than live a sorrowful widow's life without you."*

— Letter from King James to George Villiers, 1623

Historians such as David M. Bergeron and Michael B. Young have written extensively about King James' sexuality. While same-sex acts were publicly condemned in that era, the monarchy often operated above reproach, and James' affections for his male companions were well-known in court.

The irony? The Bible most often used to condemn homosexuality was commissioned by a man who very likely loved men himself.

This fact should make readers pause. If the KJV can be accepted as a sacred and trusted translation—despite the complicated, likely queer life of its patron—then surely LGBTQ+ people today are not outside the reach of divine love and inclusion.

In Summary

David and Jonathan's relationship, with its covenantal language and expressions of love, stands as one of the most emotionally powerful male-male bonds in the Bible. When viewed alongside historical truths about King James himself, the evidence is compelling: same-sex love was not erased by divine will, but by human discomfort.

When we let the scriptures speak honestly—without the lens of fear or cultural bias—we uncover a truth more beautiful and liberating than we were ever taught: **Love, in all its forms, is sacred.**

Biblical and Historical Evidence of Same-Sex Love: A Deeper Examination

Contrary to popular belief, the Bible contains multiple examples of deep, same-sex love and devotion. While modern interpretations have often ignored or erased these relationships, a closer examination of scripture reveals that love between individuals of the same gender was not condemned, but in many cases, honored and celebrated. This chapter explores some of the most notable examples, supported by biblical texts in both the King James Version (KJV) and the New International Version (NIV). Additionally, we will touch upon historical and scientific evidence regarding King James, the monarch responsible for commissioning the King James Bible, and the strong arguments that he himself was homosexual.

David and Jonathan: A Covenant of Love

One of the most intimate and powerful examples of same-sex love in the Bible is the relationship between David and Jonathan. In **1 Samuel 18:1–4**, we read about a moment of profound emotional connection that marks the beginning of their relationship:

1 Samuel 18:1-4 (KJV)

"And it came to pass, when he had made an end of speaking unto Saul, that the soul of Jonathan was knit with the soul of David, and Jonathan loved him as his own soul. And Saul took him that day, and would let him go no more home to his father's house. Then Jonathan and David made a covenant, because he loved him as his own soul. And Jonathan stripped himself of the robe that was upon him, and gave it to David, and his garments, even to his sword, and to his bow, and to his girdle."

1 Samuel 18:1-4 (NIV)

"After David had finished talking with Saul, Jonathan became one in spirit with David, and he loved him as himself. From that day Saul kept David with him and did not let him return home to his family. And Jonathan made a covenant with David because he loved him as himself. Jonathan took off the robe he was wearing and gave it to David, along with his tunic, and even his sword, his bow and his belt."

The phrase "loved him as his own soul" is used twice, emphasizing the intensity of Jonathan's feelings for David. The language here is not used elsewhere for platonic male friendships in the Bible. The act of Jonathan removing his royal garments and weapons and giving them to David symbolized a transfer of power, authority, and protection. In ancient Israel, robes and weapons represented one's identity, role, and legacy. By giving these to David, Jonathan symbolically submitted to David in a gesture that resembles marital or covenantal language.

Their love was not just personal—it had social and political ramifications. Later in **1 Samuel 20**, when Jonathan risks his life to protect David from Saul, we see a passionate goodbye between the two men:

1 Samuel 20:41 (KJV)

"They kissed one another, and wept one with another, until David exceeded."

1 Samuel 20:41 (NIV)

"Then they kissed each other and wept together—but David wept the most."

After Jonathan's death, David's grief reaches its peak in his lament:

2 Samuel 1:26 (KJV)

"I am distressed for thee, my brother Jonathan: very pleasant hast thou been unto me: thy love to me was wonderful, passing the love of women."

2 Samuel 1:26 (NIV)

"I grieve for you, Jonathan my brother; you were very dear to me. Your love for me was wonderful, more wonderful than that of women."

David, who had multiple wives, including Michal (Jonathan's sister) and Bathsheba, openly declares that Jonathan's love surpassed the love he experienced from women. The Hebrew word for "wonderful" (פָּלְא) used here denotes something extraordinary, surpassing what is normal or expected. In the original context, this was not just a poetic gesture—it was a declaration of profound, exceptional, possibly romantic love.

Ruth and Naomi: A Devotion Stronger Than Blood

The story of Ruth and Naomi is another powerful depiction of love and loyalty between two women. Ruth's devotion to Naomi is unmatched by any other relationship in the book.

Ruth 1:16–17 (KJV)

"And Ruth said, Intreat me not to leave thee, or to return from following after thee: for whither thou goest, I will go; and where thou lodgest, I will lodge: thy people shall be my people, and thy God my God: Where thou diest, will I die, and there will I be buried: the Lord do so to me, and more also, if ought but death part thee and me."

Ruth 1:16–17 (NIV)

"But Ruth replied, 'Don't urge me to leave you or to turn back from you. Where you go I will go, and where you stay I will stay. Your people will be my people and your God my God. Where you die I will die, and there I will be buried. May the Lord deal with me, be it ever so severely, if even death separates you and me.'"

This vow of loyalty, often quoted in wedding ceremonies today, was spoken between two women. While their relationship is not explicitly romantic, the emotional and spiritual commitment expressed by Ruth surpasses mere filial duty. Her decision to stay with Naomi instead of seeking a second marriage among her own people shows the strength of her attachment and possibly a deeper, enduring love.

The Centurion and His Servant: A Queer Affirmation in the Gospels

In **Matthew 8:5–13**, Jesus encounters a Roman centurion who asks Him to heal his "servant." The Greek word used here is **pais**, which often referred to a younger male companion or beloved, especially in Greco-Roman cultural contexts where pederastic relationships were known.

Matthew 8:5–7 (KJV)

"And when Jesus was entered into Capernaum, there came unto him a centurion, beseeching him, And saying, Lord, my servant lieth at home sick of the palsy, grievously tormented. And Jesus saith unto him, I will come and heal him."

Matthew 8:5–7 (NIV)

"When Jesus had entered Capernaum, a centurion came to him, asking for help. 'Lord,' he said, 'my servant lies at home paralyzed, suffering terribly.' Jesus said to him, 'Shall I come and heal him?'"

Jesus not only agrees to heal the servant but praises the centurion's faith, saying:

Matthew 8:10 (KJV)

"Verily I say unto you, I have not found so great faith, no, not in Israel."

Matthew 8:10 (NIV)

"Truly I tell you, I have not found anyone in Israel with such great faith."

There is no condemnation. No hesitation. Jesus heals the servant and affirms the centurion's love and faith. Many scholars believe the centurion-

servant relationship may have included emotional or romantic elements, particularly due to the choice of Greek terms and the centurion's desperation.

King James: The Gay Monarch Behind the Bible

The irony of how the King James Bible has been used to condemn homosexuality becomes clear when examining the life of **King James I** of England himself. Historical evidence points to his romantic relationships with men,

particularly **Robert Carr, Earl of Somerset**, and **George Villiers, Duke of Buckingham**.

In letters to Villiers, James wrote:

> "I naturally so love your person, and adore all your other parts... I desire only to live in this world for your sake."

Historians such as **David M. Bergeron**, **Michael B. Young**, and **Antonia Fraser** have affirmed the romantic undertones of these relationships. Despite the political risks, James publicly favored these men, elevating them in status and giving them power.

Yet this same man authorized the Bible translation that would later be wielded as a weapon against people like himself—a tragic contradiction fueled more by religious politics than divine truth.

Conclusion: Sacred Love Beyond Boundaries

When we look honestly at these stories—David and Jonathan, Ruth and Naomi, the Centurion and his *pais*, and even the life of King James himself—we are forced to reckon with a divine truth: **Same-sex love has always existed within the fabric of sacred history.** These bonds were not condemned—they were memorialized, respected, and in some cases, divinely affirmed.

God's love knows no boundaries. And when we silence or erase these stories, we are not protecting the Bible—we are dishonoring it.

This chapter calls us not to reinterpret the Bible, but to **reclaim** what has always been there: **proof that God made us, and loves us, exactly as we are.**

Love Has Always Been Present

Throughout the Bible, examples of same-sex devotion exist, often hidden beneath translation choices that favor heteronormative narratives. From David and Jonathan's intimate bond to Jesus' acceptance of a Roman centurion and his servant, the evidence is clear: the Bible does not condemn love, but rather celebrates it in many forms. The history of King James further highlights that even those in positions of religious authority have been part of the LGBTQ+ community.

Love is divine, and nothing can separate us from the love of God.

3

The Role of Culture in Biblical Condemnation

Many prohibitions in the Bible stem from ancient cultural norms rather than divine commands. This chapter will explore the various historical societies' perspectives on sexuality, the cultural influences that shaped modern Christian views on homosexuality, and how many contemporary prohibitions regarding same-sex relationships were not necessarily a divine command but rather the reflection of human tradition and societal norms. It will also delve into how different cultures around the world, both past and present, perceive homosexuality and the punishments that may be imposed on individuals who engage in same-sex relationships. Lastly, we will examine how modern Christian beliefs about homosexuality were not derived solely from the scriptures but from centuries of human interpretation and tradition, and why certain cultures have adhered to prohibitions in the Bible more rigidly than others.

The Ancient Perspective: Homosexuality in Early Societies

Homosexuality, far from being a modern phenomenon, has existed in numerous ancient civilizations and cultures around the world. These societies did not always perceive same-sex relationships in the same light as modern Christianity does. In many cases, these relationships were accepted or even celebrated as part of the fabric of their social and spiritual lives.

In **ancient Greece**, for instance, homosexuality was not only accepted but was integrated into the social structure, particularly in the context of mentorship and military camaraderie. It was common for older men, or *erastes*, to engage in romantic and sexual relationships with younger men, or *eromenos*. These relationships were viewed as educational and were a central feature of the social and political fabric of Greek life. In fact, the philosopher **Plato** wrote extensively about the concept of love, and while he differentiated between different kinds of love, including romantic and erotic, he acknowledged that homosexual relationships could be intellectually enriching and spiritually fulfilling.

In **ancient Rome**, same-sex relationships were also prevalent, though there were social distinctions. Roman law dictated that men should not be dominated in a sexual context, and thus the role of the "active" partner in a relationship was seen as acceptable, while the "passive" partner (often a slave or a lower-status person) was stigmatized. However, same-sex relationships were not uncommon, especially among the elite class. Roman society did not necessarily see these relationships as sinful; they were considered part of the broader range of human sexual expression, which included both heterosexual and homosexual interactions.

The **ancient Egyptians** also had a history of same-sex relationships. Evidence from the tomb of **Khnumhotep and Niankhkhnum**, two royal servants from the Fifth Dynasty, suggests that their relationship may have been romantic and sexual in nature. The pair are depicted embracing and holding hands in a highly affectionate manner, a stark contrast to the more rigid Christian views of relationships that would come centuries later.

In **ancient Mesopotamia**, sexual relationships between men were also present, though they were often tied to specific religious practices. In **Sumerian culture**, certain temple rituals involved sacred prostitution, and while these rituals were meant to honor the gods, they may also have involved same-sex relations, highlighting the spiritual connection between sexuality and religious worship. **The Code of Hammurabi** makes no explicit reference to homosexual acts, but there are indications that such relationships were generally accepted if they did not threaten the established social hierarchy.

The Role of Culture in Shaping Christian Beliefs

As Christianity spread throughout the Roman Empire and beyond, the perspectives of these ancient societies began to shift dramatically. Early Christian teachings, influenced by the moral codes of Judaism, largely rejected homosexuality, and this view became deeply embedded in the theological and social fabric of Western civilization. However, it is important to understand that many of the prohibitions against same-sex relationships in Christian theology were not derived directly from biblical scriptures, but rather from the prevailing cultural norms of the time.

Cultural norms during the early centuries of the Christian era, especially in Roman society, heavily influenced the church's stance on homosexuality. By the time Christianity became the state religion of the Roman Empire under Emperor **Constantine** in the early 4th century, social and cultural attitudes toward sex were far from neutral. Christianity, which initially adopted many of its beliefs from Judaism, inherited views of sex and sexuality that were heavily influenced by ancient Jewish laws, which prohibited homosexual acts. However, these prohibitions were not as universally pervasive in ancient societies as many believe.

In fact, it was not until the writings of early Christian theologians such as **St. Augustine of Hippo** and **St. Thomas Aquinas** in the Middle Ages that Christian doctrine began to codify the strict prohibitions against homosexuality that are still prevalent today. St. Augustine, in particular, was heavily influenced by the social norms of his time, including the Roman disdain for certain forms of sexual expression. Augustine's writings

on sexuality are characterized by an intense focus on chastity, particularly the idea that sexual activity should only occur within the context of procreation within heterosexual marriage. This perspective shaped much of Christian thought on sexuality for centuries, influencing the development of church doctrine and its condemnation of same-sex relationships.

How Culture Influenced Modern Christian Teachings on Homosexuality

In more recent history, the views of homosexuality in many Christian denominations have been shaped by traditions and cultural biases rather than a direct reading of biblical texts. In particular, much of the modern condemnation of homosexuality within Christianity stems from a specific reading of certain scriptures, including **Leviticus 18:22** ("Do not lie with a man as one lies with a woman; that is detestable") and **Romans 1:26-27**, which speaks of "unnatural" relations between men and women. However, many biblical scholars and theologians now argue that these passages were written within a cultural context that did not understand the modern concept of sexual orientation, which emerged much later.

Furthermore, many of the biblical prohibitions against homosexuality stem from **ancient Jewish cultural norms**. For instance, the Book of Leviticus, which contains several laws on morality and ritual purity, was written in a time when cultural norms were largely centered around maintaining ethnic purity and distinguishing Israelite practices from those of their neighbors. Many of the laws in Leviticus were about setting boundaries that differentiated the Israelites from the surrounding nations, and the prohibition against homosexual acts was in many ways a reaction to the practices of other ancient societies.

Punishments for Homosexuality: Then and Now

In many cultures throughout history, homosexuality has been punishable by severe penalties. In ancient **Rome**, for example, while homosexual relationships were tolerated, the laws still placed certain restrictions on who could engage in them and under what circumstances. Homosexual acts between free men were often seen as a violation of Roman masculinity and were therefore stigmatized. In contrast, slavery in Rome allowed for sexual relations between masters and slaves, including same-sex encounters, though the master was expected to maintain his role as the dominant partner.

In **medieval Europe**, during the height of the Inquisition, homosexual acts were often viewed as crimes against God and nature. Those found guilty of engaging in same-sex relations were subject to extreme forms of punishment, including imprisonment, execution by burning, or being stoned to death. The rise of the **Catholic Church** during this period solidified these views, and homosexuality was often equated with heresy.

In modern times, certain cultures and countries still impose severe punishments on those found guilty of homosexuality. For example, in several **Middle Eastern countries**, such as **Saudi Arabia**, **Iran**, and **Yemen**, homosexual acts are punishable by death. These laws are often rooted in a blend of **Islamic** teachings and ancient cultural practices. Similarly, in some **African** nations, such as **Uganda** and **Nigeria**, homosexuality is considered illegal and can result in lengthy prison sentences or even death, reflecting a mix of **Christian** and **Islamic** influences on the region's laws.

Cultural Shunning and Religious Exclusion

Several religions, particularly those with conservative interpretations, still shun individuals who identify as homosexual. **Islam**, with its teachings grounded in the Quran and Hadith, generally condemns homosexual acts, viewing them as sinful and unnatural. The Quran does not mention homosexuality explicitly, but it alludes to the people of **Lut** (Lot), whose story is often interpreted as condemning same-sex relations. As a result, many Islamic countries maintain legal prohibitions against homosexuality and ostracize individuals who engage in such acts.

Judaism, particularly Orthodox Judaism, similarly condemns homosexuality based on interpretations of the Torah, specifically **Leviticus 18:22**. In contrast, more liberal branches of Judaism, such as **Reform** and **Conservative Judaism**, have become more accepting of same-sex relationships and have granted full participation in religious life to LGBTQ+ individuals.

In certain **Christian** denominations, particularly the **Roman Catholic Church**, **Southern Baptist Convention**, and other evangelical Protestant groups, homosexuality is still viewed as a sin. These groups often argue that biblical texts explicitly condemn same-sex acts, and individuals who identify as LGBTQ+ are often excommunicated or shunned. However, progressive Christian communities have increasingly adopted a more inclusive approach, interpreting the Bible in ways that affirm LGBTQ+ rights and relationships.

Conclusion

The condemnation of homosexuality in the Bible and modern Christian thought is not as straightforward as it may appear. The prohibition of same-sex relationships was shaped by ancient cultural norms rather than a direct divine command. The evolution of Christian doctrine, influenced by societal views and religious leaders throughout history, has cemented a view of homosexuality as sinful, yet this is not the sole interpretation of the Bible. Cultures around the world, both past and present, have viewed homosexuality in various ways, and many societies were much more accepting of same-sex relationships than modern Western Christianity often acknowledges. It is important to recognize that the condemnation of homosexuality in many modern religious and cultural contexts reflects long-standing human traditions rather than the intent of divine scripture.

4

Same-Sex Love

Before the Bible

Same-sex relationships existed long before the Bible was written. From ancient Mesopotamia and Egypt to the love poetry of Sappho in Greece, historical records prove that same-sex love has always been a part of humanity. The idea that homosexuality is a modern phenomenon or a product of recent cultural shifts is contradicted by ample historical evidence. This chapter delves into documented cases of same-sex love from different civilizations, showing that such relationships were not only present but, in many cases, acknowledged, celebrated, or institutionalized long before biblical texts were written.

Same-Sex Relationships in Ancient Mesopotamia

The civilizations of Mesopotamia (modern-day Iraq, Iran, Syria, and Turkey) were among the earliest to record human history, dating back over 5,000 years. In Sumerian and Akkadian texts, references to same-sex relationships are found in myths, legal codes, and personal correspondence.

One of the earliest documented cases comes from the **Epic of Gilgamesh**, written around 2100 BCE. The story revolves around the deep bond between King Gilgamesh and Enkidu. While interpretations vary, their relationship has been described as more than just friendship, with some scholars arguing that it includes romantic and possibly sexual undertones. The intensity of their connection is evident in the grief-stricken lamentations of Gilgamesh after Enkidu's death, which resemble the loss of a spouse rather than a mere companion.

The Mesopotamian pantheon also included **same-sex deities** and gender-fluid figures. The goddess **Inanna (Ishtar)**, the deity of love and fertility, was closely associated with the *gala* priests, who were believed to be involved in same-sex relationships and possibly transgender identities. These priests played important roles in temple rituals, suggesting that diverse expressions of gender and sexuality were recognized and even considered sacred in Mesopotamian culture.

Ancient Egypt and Same-Sex Love

Ancient Egyptian civilization, which flourished along the Nile for thousands of years, also provides evidence of same-sex relationships.

One of the most famous examples comes from the tomb of **Khnumhotep and Niankhkhnum**, two high-ranking officials who lived during the Fifth Dynasty (circa 2400 BCE).

Their tomb depicts them embracing and holding hands in intimate poses commonly reserved for married couples. While some scholars argue that they were brothers, others suggest that they were lovers, given the affectionate nature of their portrayal.

Egyptian mythology also includes references to same-sex relationships among the gods. **Horus and Seth**, two prominent deities, were involved in a mythological episode in which Seth attempted to assert dominance over Horus by engaging in a sexual act. While the story is often interpreted as a struggle for power rather than an expression of love, it nonetheless demonstrates an awareness of same-sex interactions in ancient Egyptian thought.

Additionally, love poetry from ancient Egypt includes homoerotic themes. Some poems express deep affection and longing between people of the same sex, providing insight into the existence of same-sex desire within Egyptian society.

Greece: Sappho and the Institutionalized Same-Sex Love

Ancient Greece is perhaps one of the most well-documented cultures when it comes to same-sex relationships. **Sappho of Lesbos (circa 630-570 BCE)** is one of the most famous figures in this context. A poet from the island of Lesbos, Sappho wrote passionate and evocative poetry about love and desire between women. Her poetry, which inspired the term "lesbian," celebrated deep romantic and erotic connections between women. Although much of her work has been lost, fragments remain that speak openly of her longing for female lovers:

"Sweet mother, I cannot weave— Slender Aphrodite has overcome me With longing for a girl."

Same-sex relationships among men were also institutionalized in Greek society. The practice of **pederasty**, a socially recognized bond between an older man (*erastes*) and a younger male (*eromenos*), was a structured part of education and mentorship. Philosophers such as **Plato** wrote extensively about love between men, particularly in his dialogue *Symposium*, where different perspectives on love are discussed. Plato's *Phaedrus* even suggests that same-sex love is superior to heterosexual love in its pursuit of intellectual and spiritual fulfillment.

Same-Sex Relationships in Asia

In **ancient China**, homosexuality was often referred to as the "passion of the cut sleeve" (*duanxiu zhi pi*), a term originating from Emperor Ai of Han (27–1 BCE). According to historical records, the emperor had a male lover, Dong Xian, whom he adored so much that when Dong fell asleep on his sleeve, Ai cut off his own sleeve rather than disturb him.

Same-sex relationships were widely accepted in Chinese culture, especially among the upper classes. The **Poet Ruan Ji (210–263 CE)** and later literary figures wrote about male love. Historical records show that numerous emperors and high-ranking officials engaged in same-sex relationships without stigma.

Similarly, in **Japan**, **samurai culture** included male-male relationships known as **wakashudō** ("the way of the youth"). This practice was similar to Greek pederasty, where younger men trained under older samurai, forming close personal and sometimes sexual relationships. Buddhist monks in medieval Japan also documented same-sex attraction in temple life.

Same-Sex Love in the Indigenous Cultures of the Americas

Among Indigenous cultures in North and South America, gender and sexuality were understood in diverse ways.

Many Indigenous North American tribes recognized **Two-Spirit** people—individuals who embodied both masculine and feminine traits. Two-Spirit individuals often took on spiritual or leadership roles within their communities and engaged in same-sex relationships.

In South America, the **Moche civilization** (100-700 CE) in Peru produced pottery depicting explicit same-sex acts, suggesting that these relationships were acknowledged, if not celebrated. The artwork indicates that non-heterosexual relationships were part of the natural human experience long before European colonization introduced Christian prohibitions.

Same-Sex Relationships in Africa

In **pre-colonial Africa**, same-sex relationships were common in several societies. The **Dagaaba people of Ghana and Burkina Faso** had traditions recognizing same-sex partnerships, and among the **Igbo of Nigeria**, female-female marriages were historically practiced to ensure lineage continuation. The **Buganda kingdom (modern Uganda)** had openly gay monarchs, such as King Mwanga II, who defied European missionaries' attempts to impose Christian morality.

Conclusion: A History Erased and Rewritten

The historical evidence of same-sex love across cultures and centuries challenges the notion that homosexuality is unnatural or a modern invention. These relationships existed long before the Bible was written, often being accepted, celebrated, or institutionalized in various societies. The advent of Abrahamic religions, particularly Christianity and Islam, reshaped attitudes toward same-sex love, often condemning what was once tolerated or revered.

By recognizing the historical presence of same-sex relationships, we dismantle the argument that homosexuality is a deviation from tradition.

Instead, we see that the suppression of LGBTQ+ identities is a relatively recent imposition shaped by specific cultural and religious shifts rather than divine mandate. Understanding this history allows us to reframe modern discussions about same-sex love in a way that acknowledges its enduring role in human civilization.

5

How Different Cultures View
Same-Sex Relationships

While Christianity has often been a driving force behind anti-LGBTQ+ laws, many cultures have embraced same-sex love throughout history. This chapter highlights societies that revered LGBTQ+ individuals, including Indigenous Two-Spirit people, same-sex marriages in ancient Africa, and the hijras of South Asia.

Christianity's Role in Anti-LGBTQ+ Laws

Throughout history, Christianity has played a significant role in shaping laws and social attitudes against same-sex relationships. Many of these laws stem not from biblical commands but from human interpretations influenced by cultural biases. Theologians and religious leaders have historically used scripture to justify discrimination, despite the Bible lacking explicit condemnations of consensual same-sex relationships in the way modern anti-LGBTQ+ rhetoric suggests.

Biblical Passages Used Against LGBTQ+ People

Opponents of same-sex relationships often cite a ha

ndful of biblical passages to justify their stance. However, historical and linguistic studies show that many of these passages were either mistranslated or taken out of their original cultural context. Below are some of the most frequently cited verses, with full texts from the **King James Version (KJV)** and **New International Version (NIV)** for comparison:

Leviticus 18:22

- **KJV**: "Thou shalt not lie with mankind, as with womankind: it is abomination."

- **NIV**: "Do not have sexual relations with a man as one does with a woman; that is detestable."

Leviticus 20:13

- **KJV**: "If a man also lie with mankind, as he lieth with a woman, both of them have committed an abomination: they shall surely be put to death; their blood shall be upon them."

- **NIV**: "If a man has sexual relations with a man as one does with a woman, both of them have done what is detestable. They are to be put to death; their blood will be on their own heads."

[

Romans 1:26-27

- **KJV**: "For this cause God gave them up unto vile affections: for even their women did change the natural use into that which is against nature: And likewise also the men, leaving the natural use of the woman, burned in their lust one toward another; men with men working that which is unseemly, and receiving in themselves that recompence of their error which was meet."

- **NIV**: "Because of this, God gave them over to shameful lusts. Even their women exchanged natural sexual relations for unnatural ones. In the same way the men also abandoned natural relations with women and were inflamed with lust for one another. Men committed shameful acts with other men, and received in themselves the due penalty for their error."

Cultural and Historical Context of These Verses

It is important to note that the Hebrew word translated as "abomination" in Leviticus is "toevah," which refers to ritual impurity, not an inherent moral failing. The prohibitions in Leviticus are part of the Holiness Code, meant to distinguish Israelites from surrounding pagan cultures rather than dictate universal moral law. Additionally, Paul's writings in Romans were directed at specific practices in Roman temple prostitution, not loving same-sex relationships.

Man's Influence on Christian Teachings About Homosexuality

Many Christian doctrines about sexuality developed not from scripture but from cultural beliefs and biases. The influence of Greek and Roman philosophers like Aristotle and Plato, who viewed procreation as the sole purpose of sex, shaped early Christian thought. By the time of **Augustine of Hippo (354–430 CE)**, church teachings had solidified around the idea that non-procreative sex was sinful.

During the **Middle Ages**, Christian leaders imposed severe penalties for homosexuality, drawing more from legal codes than biblical commandments. The **Buggery Act of 1533** in England, introduced under Henry VIII, criminalized sodomy with the death penalty. Similar laws spread throughout European colonies, embedding anti-LGBTQ+ sentiment in legal systems worldwide.

Cultures That Revered LGBTQ+ Individuals

Contrary to the idea that same-sex love is a modern concept, numerous cultures throughout history have embraced or even revered LGBTQ+ individuals.

Two-Spirit People of Indigenous North America

The term **Two-Spirit** is used by many Indigenous peoples in North America to describe individuals who embody both masculine and feminine spirits. Before European colonization, Two-Spirit people were often honored as healers, spiritual leaders, and warriors.

Among the **Lakota, Zuni, and Navajo** tribes, Two-Spirit individuals held sacred roles in ceremonies and community life. They were seen as possessing unique spiritual insight, and their relationships with both men and women were widely accepted. It was only after the imposition of Christian values during colonization that Two-Spirit identities were stigmatized.

Same-Sex Marriages in Pre-Colonial Africa

Many African cultures recognized same-sex relationships before the arrival of European colonialism. In several societies, female-female marriages were not only accepted but legally and culturally recognized.

For example, among the **Igbo people of Nigeria**, women could marry other women to continue their lineage if they could not bear children. This practice had no connection to modern Western definitions of lesbianism but demonstrated a cultural understanding that gender roles could be fluid.

Similarly, in the **Dahomey Kingdom (now Benin)**, royal courts included homosexual and gender-nonconforming individuals who held high-status positions. **King Mwanga II of Buganda (Uganda)**, in the 19th century, was known for having male lovers, a practice that was accepted until European missionaries condemned it.

Hijras of South Asia

In South Asia, **Hijras** have been recognized for thousands of years as a third gender. Traditionally, Hijras are transgender, intersex, or eunuch individuals who often serve as spiritual figures, performing blessings at births and weddings.

Ancient Hindu texts, such as the **Ramayana and the Kama Sutra**, reference same-sex relationships and gender variance. In Hinduism, several deities, including **Shiva and Vishnu**, are depicted as gender-fluid or engaging in same-sex relationships. Colonial-era laws, such as **Section 377 of the Indian Penal Code**, imposed European homophobia on the region, criminalizing same-sex intimacy until its repeal in 2018.

Modern Resistance to LGBTQ+ Acceptance

Despite historical evidence of LGBTQ+ acceptance, Christianity continues to be a major force behind anti-LGBTQ+ policies. Many conservative Christian groups advocate against LGBTQ+ rights based on doctrine shaped by human biases rather than scripture.

However, there is also growing recognition among Christian scholars that the Bible does not condemn loving, committed same-sex relationships. Movements such as **progressive Christianity** and **queer theology** challenge traditional interpretations, advocating for an inclusive understanding of scripture.

Conclusion: Returning to a More Inclusive Understanding

The narrative that homosexuality is unnatural or solely a modern Western concept is contradicted by history. Numerous cultures have celebrated and honored LGBTQ+ individuals long before Christianity imposed restrictive doctrines. By understanding these histories, we can challenge the belief that anti-LGBTQ+ sentiment is inherent to faith and instead recognize that it is a product of human interpretation and cultural shifts, not divine command.

6

The Christian Origins of Anti-LGBTQ+ Beliefs

Anti-homosexuality rhetoric is not rooted in scripture but in the political and social ambitions of religious leaders. This chapter traces the historical shift in Christian doctrine, showing how church leaders manipulated religious texts to enforce conformity and control sexuality.

The Political and Social Ambitions Behind Anti-LGBTQ+ Teachings

The condemnation of same-sex relationships in Christianity was not inherent to the early faith but emerged as church leaders sought to consolidate power, enforce social order, and control human sexuality. Throughout history, religious leaders have manipulated scripture and doctrine to suit their political agendas, often using homophobia as a tool to maintain authority.

One of the earliest examples of this can be seen in the Roman Empire's adoption of Christianity as a state religion. **Emperor Constantine** (272–337 CE), after converting to Christianity, sought to unify his empire under a single religious doctrine. While early Christian communities were diverse in belief and practice, Constantine and later rulers promoted a more rigid, hierarchical version of Christianity that aligned with the empire's political interests. This included reinforcing strict gender roles and controlling sexuality, which meant condemning any behavior that challenged procreative, heterosexual marriage.

The Shift in Christian Doctrine on Homosexuality

Early Christianity was heavily influenced by Greco-Roman culture, where same-sex relationships were widely accepted, particularly among the elite. Many early Christian texts do not mention homosexuality at all, and those that do have been mistranslated or misinterpreted over time. It was not until the Middle Ages that anti-homosexuality teachings became a central focus of Christian morality.

Augustine of Hippo and the War on Desire

One of the most influential figures in shaping Christian doctrine on sexuality was **St. Augustine of Hippo (354–430 CE)**. Augustine's writings on sin, particularly in *Confessions*, laid the groundwork for Christian sexual ethics. He taught that all sexual desire was inherently sinful unless it was

strictly for procreation within marriage. This belief extended to same-sex relationships, which were condemned not because of biblical command but because they did not result in reproduction.

Augustine's teachings influenced later theologians, including **Thomas Aquinas (1225–1274)**, who categorized homosexuality as "unnatural" in his *Summa Theologica*. Aquinas relied on **Aristotle's philosophy**, which taught that sex should serve a biological function. By equating natural law with divine law, Aquinas and other church leaders created a theological framework that condemned same-sex love without biblical justification.

The Role of the Catholic Church in Anti-LGBTQ+ Rhetoric

During the **Medieval period**, the Catholic Church intensified its stance against same-sex relationships, using it as a means to exert control over clergy and laypeople alike.

- **Canon law**: By the 12th century, sodomy was declared a sin punishable by excommunication, and by the **13th century**, it became a criminal offense in many Christian territories.

- **The Inquisition**: During the Spanish Inquisition (1478–1834), accusations of sodomy were used to target political enemies and enforce religious conformity. Many individuals were tortured and executed based on mere suspicion of engaging in same-sex relationships.

- **The Witch Hunts**: In the **16th and 17th centuries**, women accused of witchcraft were often believed to have engaged in "unnatural acts," including lesbianism. Homosexuality was linked to heresy, further demonizing LGBTQ+ individuals.

Self-Hatred and the Anti-LGBTQ+ Teachings of Religious Leaders

History has shown that some of the most vocal religious leaders against homosexuality struggled with their own same-sex attractions. This self-hatred often fueled extreme anti-LGBTQ+ rhetoric.

Pope Paul IV (1476–1559)

Pope Paul IV, who strengthened the Church's opposition to same-sex relationships, was rumored to have engaged in relationships with young men while condemning homosexuality as a mortal sin. His personal struggles with sexuality likely played a role in his harsh policies.

J. Edgar Hoover (1895–1972)

Though not a religious figure, **J. Edgar Hoover**, the first director of the FBI, was a deeply religious man who aligned with conservative Christian values.

He was notorious for persecuting LGBTQ+ individuals, yet historical evidence suggests he was involved in same-sex relationships. Hoover's personal fears and self-hatred contributed to his aggressive anti-LGBTQ+ policies, showing a broader pattern in which leaders project their insecurities onto others.

Mistranslations and Biblical Manipulations to Justify Homophobia

Many verses commonly used to condemn homosexuality were either mistranslated or taken out of context. Here are a few examples:

1 Corinthians 6:9-10

- **KJV**: "Know ye not that the unrighteous shall not inherit the kingdom of God? Be not deceived: neither fornicators, nor idolaters, nor adulterers, nor effeminate, nor abusers of themselves with mankind."

- **NIV**: "Or do you not know that wrongdoers will not inherit the kingdom of God? Do not be deceived: Neither the sexually immoral nor idolaters nor adulterers nor men who have sex with men."

The phrase **"abusers of themselves with mankind"** in the KJV was translated from the Greek word **arsenokoitai**, which does not directly refer to homosexuality. Scholars suggest it refers to economic exploitation or abuse, not loving same-sex relationships.

Christianity's Influence on Anti-LGBTQ+ Laws Worldwide

As European colonial powers spread Christianity around the world, they also exported homophobic laws and attitudes.

- **Britain**: The **Buggery Act of 1533**, introduced under Henry VIII, criminalized sodomy, setting a precedent for anti-LGBTQ+ laws in British colonies.

- **The United States**: Many early American laws against homosexuality were based on Puritan religious beliefs. Even today, anti-LGBTQ+ laws are often justified using Christian rhetoric.

- **Africa**: Before colonialism, many African societies accepted same-sex relationships. However, European missionaries imposed Christian teachings that labeled homosexuality as sinful, leading to modern anti-LGBTQ+ laws in countries like Uganda and Nigeria.

Cultures That Embraced Same-Sex Love

Despite the Church's efforts, many cultures historically embraced same-sex relationships. These include:

- **The Native American Two-Spirit tradition**: Revered as spiritual leaders.

- **Ancient Rome and Greece**: Where male-male and female-female relationships were widely accepted.

- **Japan's Samurai Culture**: Same-sex relationships among samurai were considered a bond of honor.

- **The Ottoman Empire**: Where same-sex relationships were often depicted in poetry and art.

Conclusion: A Manufactured Doctrine

The belief that Christianity has always condemned same-sex love is historically inaccurate. The shift toward homophobia was a result of human ambition, social control, and political strategy, rather than divine command. By understanding the historical manipulation of scripture, we can challenge modern anti-LGBTQ+ rhetoric and reclaim an inclusive interpretation of faith that embraces all of God's creations.

7

The Science and Nature of Same-Sex Love

Nature itself reveals the normalcy of same-sex love. This chapter presents scientific evidence, including studies on animal behavior, human psychology, and genetics, that prove being LGBTQ+ is a natural and inherent part of life.

Same-Sex Love in the Animal Kingdom

One of the strongest pieces of evidence proving the natural occurrence of same-sex love is found in the animal kingdom. Numerous scientific studies have documented homosexual behavior in more than **1,500 animal species**, from mammals and birds to insects and fish. This demonstrates that same-sex attraction is not a human invention but an inherent part of life on Earth.

Notable Examples of Same-Sex Behavior in Animals

- **Penguins**: Many zoos have documented same-sex penguin pairs. In 1999, two male chinstrap penguins, **Roy and Silo**, at New York's Central Park Zoo formed a pair bond, incubated an egg together, and raised a chick named Tango. Similar cases have been observed in various penguin species around the world.

- **Bonobos**: These great apes, closely related to humans, engage in same-sex relations as a way of bonding, conflict resolution, and pleasure. Female bonobos frequently engage in **genito-genital rubbing**, while males participate in **penis-fencing** to strengthen social connections.

- **Dolphins**: Male bottlenose dolphins often form same-sex pair bonds that last for years. They engage in sexual behaviors that reinforce their social structure and maintain lifelong companionships.

- **Giraffes**: Research shows that over **90% of observed sexual activity** in giraffes occurs between males. These interactions establish dominance and form strong social bonds.

• **Lions**: Male lions have been observed engaging in affectionate behaviors, including mounting and nuzzling, forming long-lasting partnerships with other males.

These examples highlight that same-sex attraction and behavior are deeply ingrained in nature, not deviations or "unnatural" occurrences as some claim.

Genetic and Biological Basis of Sexual Orientation

Scientific research has shown that sexual orientation is not a choice but an innate aspect of human biology. Several studies point to genetic, hormonal, and neurological factors that influence same-sex attraction.

Genetic Studies on Sexual Orientation

• **Twin Studies**: Studies on identical twins have found that if one twin is gay, the other has a much higher chance of also being gay compared to non-identical twins, suggesting a genetic component.

• **X Chromosome Link**: Research from the **National Institute for Mathematical and Biological Synthesis** has found a link between male homosexuality and the **Xq28 region** of the X chromosome, inherited from the mother.

• **Family Patterns**: Studies show that homosexuality tends to run in families, reinforcing the idea that genetic factors influence sexual orientation.

Hormonal Influences on Sexual Orientation

• **Prenatal Hormones**: Exposure to different levels of testosterone and estrogen in the womb can affect sexual orientation. Studies suggest that the brains of gay men and straight women share structural similarities, while lesbians and straight men have similar brain structures.

● **The Fraternal Birth Order Effect**: Research shows that men with older brothers are more likely to be gay. This is believed to be due to changes in a mother's immune system that affect male fetal development.

Psychological and Sociological Evidence for LGBTQ+ Normalcy

Modern psychology recognizes that being LGBTQ+ is a natural variation of human sexuality, not a disorder. The **American Psychiatric Association (APA)** removed homosexuality from the **Diagnostic and Statistical Manual of Mental Disorders (DSM)** in 1973, acknowledging that same-sex attraction is not pathological.

● **Studies on LGBTQ+ Mental Health**: Psychological research confirms that the mental health struggles experienced by many LGBTQ+ individuals result from societal discrimination, not from their sexual orientation itself.

● **Cross-Cultural Acceptance of Same-Sex Love**: Many cultures throughout history have embraced LGBTQ+ individuals without stigma. Cultures that accept same-sex love tend to have lower rates of mental health issues among LGBTQ+ populations, reinforcing that discrimination—not sexual orientation—is the problem.

Same-Sex Love in Cultures Around the World

Many societies have celebrated same-sex relationships and LGBTQ+ individuals as spiritual leaders, warriors, and cultural icons.

Indigenous Two-Spirit People (North America)

Many Indigenous tribes in North America recognized and revered **Two-Spirit** people—individuals who embodied both masculine and feminine qualities. Rather than seeing them as deviant, these societies honored them as spiritual leaders, healers, and visionaries.

- **The Lakota, Navajo, and Ojibwe** tribes had specific roles for Two-Spirit individuals, who often performed both male and female duties.

- **Two-Spirit people** were seen as gifted, with special insight and wisdom.

- Colonization and Christian missionaries attempted to erase this tradition, replacing Indigenous gender diversity with strict binary roles.

Same-Sex Marriages in Ancient Africa

Before colonialism imposed Western homophobia, many African societies embraced same-sex relationships.

- **Women-Women Marriages**: The **Igbo people** of Nigeria and the **Kikuyu of Kenya** practiced woman-to-woman marriage, in which a woman could take a wife for companionship, status, or inheritance purposes.

- **The Shona and Zulu Peoples**: Historical records document same-sex relationships among warriors and spiritual leaders.

Colonial rule and Christian missionaries labeled these practices "unnatural," leading to the modern-day criminalization of LGBTQ+ identities in many African nations.

The Hijras of South Asia

In **India, Pakistan, and Bangladesh**, the **Hijra** community has existed for thousands of years as a recognized third gender. Many Hijras are transgender, intersex, or gender-nonconforming individuals who often form close relationships with men.

- Ancient Hindu texts reference **Hijras as sacred beings** blessed by the gods.

- The **Kama Sutra**, written over 2,000 years ago, openly discusses same-sex relationships and non-binary genders.

- During British colonial rule, Hijras were criminalized, but today, they are legally recognized in countries like India and Nepal.

Scientific Consensus on the Normalcy of LGBTQ+ Identities

Major scientific and medical organizations affirm that LGBTQ+ identities are a natural part of human diversity:

- The **American Psychological Association (APA)** states that being LGBTQ+ is "a normal and positive variation of human sexuality."

- The **World Health Organization (WHO)** removed homosexuality from its list of mental disorders in 1992.

- The **American Academy of Pediatrics** supports LGBTQ+ youth and calls for the end of conversion therapy, which has been proven to be harmful and ineffective.

Conclusion: LGBTQ+ Identities Are Natural and Valid

The overwhelming evidence from **biology, psychology, history, and anthropology** proves that same-sex love and diverse gender identities have always existed as part of the natural world. The idea that homosexuality is "unnatural" or "sinful" is a product of **cultural bias and religious manipulation**, not scientific truth.

From the animal kingdom to ancient civilizations, same-sex love has always been a fundamental part of life. Embracing LGBTQ+ identities is not about rejecting tradition but about returning to a more inclusive and accepting view of humanity—one that nature itself supports.

8

Influential Same-Sex Couples in History

From **Alexander the Great and Hephaestion** to **Eleanor Roosevelt and Lorena Hickok**, history is filled with powerful same-sex couples whose love and partnerships changed the world. Their stories challenge the false narrative that same-sex relationships are "modern inventions" or "Western ideologies." Love transcends gender and has always played a vital role in shaping history.

Ancient and Classical Influential Same-Sex Couples

Alexander the Great and Hephaestion

The bond between **Alexander the Great** and **Hephaestion** was one of history's most famous same-sex relationships. Hephaestion was Alexander's closest companion, general, and lover. The two were inseparable, much like the legendary Greek lovers Achilles and Patroclus.

- When Hephaestion died, Alexander was devastated and declared a period of mourning.

- He arranged an elaborate funeral and sought divine honors for Hephaestion.

- Historians like Plutarch and Arrian documented their profound relationship, with Alexander often referring to Hephaestion as "another self."

Hadrian and Antinous

Roman Emperor **Hadrian** and his beloved **Antinous** had a relationship that shaped Roman culture.

- When Antinous tragically drowned in the Nile in 130 CE, Hadrian **deified him**, establishing a widespread cult in his honor.

- Cities and temples were built in Antinous' name, proving how deeply their love influenced Roman history.

Achilles and Patroclus

In **Homer's Iliad**, the relationship between Achilles and Patroclus has been widely interpreted as romantic. While some later scholars tried to downplay the nature of their love, ancient Greeks saw them as lovers.

- **Plato**, in his Symposium, referenced them as an idealized love between warriors.

- Their deep affection was recognized in art, literature, and philosophy for centuries.

Same-Sex Love in Politics and Royalty

King James I and George Villiers

King **James I of England** (1567–1625), who authorized the **King James Bible**, had a well-documented love affair with **George Villiers, Duke of Buckingham**.

- Love letters between James and Villiers reveal intimate expressions of affection.

- James referred to Villiers as "my sweetheart" and "my husband."

- Historians confirm that their relationship was romantic and had political influence.

Eleanor Roosevelt and Lorena Hickok

First Lady **Eleanor Roosevelt** had a decades-long intimate relationship with **Lorena Hickok**, a prominent journalist.

- Over **3,000 love letters** between them reveal their deep emotional and romantic connection.

- Lorena had private access to the White House and often advised Eleanor on political matters.

Eleanor's advocacy for civil rights and social justice was, in part, influenced by her personal experiences and relationships.

Baron Friedrich von Steuben and His Companions

Baron **Friedrich von Steuben**, a key figure in shaping the **U.S. military** during the Revolutionary War, was openly gay. His military prowess helped the Continental Army defeat the British.

- Von Steuben never married but lived with **his younger companions**, including his aides-de-camp.

- His legacy remains foundational in the structure of the U.S. military, despite attempts to erase his sexuality.

Hollywood, Media, and Arts: Same-Sex Love in the Spotlight

Greta Garbo and Mercedes de Acosta

Hollywood legend **Greta Garbo** had a well-known romantic relationship with writer **Mercedes de Acosta**.

- Their letters, filled with passion, demonstrate their deep bond.

- Acosta was known as the "lover of the most beautiful women in Hollywood," with relationships including **Marlene Dietrich** and **Isadora Duncan**.

Rock Hudson and Marc Christian

Leading man **Rock Hudson**, one of the biggest stars of Hollywood's golden age, had relationships hidden from the public due to Hollywood's homophobia.

- Hudson's relationship with **Marc Christian** was significant but kept secret until after his death.

- His battle with AIDS helped humanize the epidemic and shift public perceptions about LGBTQ+ individuals.

Same-Sex Love in Sports and the Military

Billie Jean King and Ilana Kloss

Tennis legend **Billie Jean King**, a trailblazer for gender equality in sports, has been in a long-term relationship with **Ilana Kloss**.

- King's advocacy for women's rights and LGBTQ+ inclusion in sports has made her one of the most influential athletes of all time.

- She was one of the first major athletes to be publicly outed and has since become a champion for equality.

Megan Rapinoe and Sue Bird

Soccer star **Megan Rapinoe** and basketball legend **Sue Bird** are one of today's most visible same-sex power couples in sports.

- Both are Olympic gold medalists and advocates for LGBTQ+ rights.

- Their visibility has helped normalize same-sex relationships in professional sports.

Same-Sex Love in Government and Politics Today

Pete Buttigieg and Chasten Buttigieg

Former presidential candidate and current **U.S. Secretary of Transportation Pete Buttigieg** is married to **Chasten Buttigieg**.

- Pete became the **first openly gay presidential candidate** to win delegates in a U.S. primary election.

- Their relationship represents a new era of LGBTQ+ representation in government.

Jóhanna Sigurðardóttir and Jónína Leósdóttir

Jóhanna Sigurðardóttir, former **Prime Minister of Iceland**, was the first openly gay world leader.

- She married **Jónína Leósdóttir**, her longtime partner, when same-sex marriage was legalized in Iceland.

- Her leadership helped push progressive policies and LGBTQ+ rights worldwide.

Conclusion: Same-Sex Love Has Always Existed and Changed the World

History proves that same-sex love has always been a fundamental part of human existence. From ancient warriors and emperors to modern politicians and athletes, LGBTQ+ relationships have shaped **politics, culture, and society**.

Despite attempts to erase or hide these relationships, love has always found a way to thrive. These couples serve as a testament to the resilience, power, and beauty of same-sex love throughout history.

9

Finding Reconciliation Between Faith and Identity

For many LGBTQ+ individuals, the journey of faith is complicated by religious teachings that seem to reject their identity. However, countless LGBTQ+ Christians have discovered peace and reconciliation, realizing that their love and faith are not mutually exclusive. This chapter explores theological perspectives, personal testimonies, and guidance for those seeking to harmonize their faith and identity.

Understanding the Struggle

For centuries, many religious institutions have misinterpreted scripture to condemn same-sex relationships and gender diversity. This has led to internal conflict for LGBTQ+ believers who feel drawn to their faith but are told they must choose between who they are and what they believe.

The heart of this struggle lies in the question: Can one be both LGBTQ+ and a faithful Christian? The answer is a resounding yes. As we have explored throughout this book, the Bible does not explicitly condemn loving same-sex relationships. Instead, much of the opposition comes from cultural traditions and human interpretations rather than divine commandments.

Theological Perspectives on LGBTQ+ Acceptance

Many theologians and progressive Christian leaders argue that LGBTQ+ people are fully embraced by God. Some key theological perspectives that affirm this belief include:

Imago Dei – Made in the Image of God

Genesis 1:27 (KJV): "So God created man in his own image, in the image of God created he him; male and female created he them."

Genesis 1:27 (NIV): "So God created mankind in his own image, in the image of God he created them; male and female he created them."

This means that all people, including LGBTQ+ individuals, are created in the divine image and are worthy of love and dignity.

The Greatest Commandment – Love Above All Else

Matthew 22:37-39 (KJV): "Jesus said unto him, Thou shalt love the Lord thy God with all thy heart, and with all thy soul, and with all thy mind.

This is the first and great commandment. And the second is like unto it, Thou shalt love thy neighbour as thyself."

Matthew 22:37-39 (NIV): "Jesus replied: 'Love the Lord your God with all your heart and with all your soul and with all your mind. This is the first and greatest commandment. And the second is like it: Love your neighbor as yourself.'"

There is no stipulation that this love must conform to specific gender norms or sexual orientations.

The Story of David and Jonathan – A Biblical Example of Same-Sex Love

1 Samuel 18:1-4 (KJV): "And it came to pass, when he had made an end of speaking unto Saul, that the soul of Jonathan was knit with the soul of David, and Jonathan loved him as his own soul."

1 Samuel 18:1-4 (NIV): "After David had finished talking with Saul, Jonathan became one in spirit with David, and he loved him as himself."

Their relationship demonstrates a deep, covenantal love, one that many scholars suggest goes beyond friendship.

Eunuchs in the Bible – A Case for Gender Diversity

Matthew 19:12 (KJV): "For there are some eunuchs, which were so born from their mother's womb: and there are some eunuchs, which were made eunuchs of men: and there be eunuchs, which have made themselves eunuchs for the kingdom of heaven's sake. He that is able to receive it, let him receive it."

Matthew 19:12 (NIV): "For there are eunuchs who were born that way, and there are eunuchs who have been made eunuchs by others—and there are those who choose to live like eunuchs for the sake of the kingdom of heaven. The one who can accept this should accept it."

This passage has been interpreted as Jesus recognizing the existence of people who do not fit traditional gender roles.

Personal Testimonies from LGBTQ+ Christians

Hearing from those who have walked this path can provide comfort and hope. Here are a few inspiring testimonies from LGBTQ+ Christians who have found reconciliation between their faith and identity.

1. **Justin Lee – Founder of the Gay Christian Network** *"I spent years wrestling with what it meant to be both gay and Christian. But as I studied scripture, I realized that God's love was bigger than any human restriction. Today, I live authentically as the person God made me to be, knowing that my faith is stronger because of it."*
2. **Vicky Beeching – Christian Singer and LGBTQ+ Advocate** *"Coming out as gay was the hardest thing I ever did, but it was also the most freeing. My faith didn't leave me—it deepened. I finally understood what it meant to live in truth and grace."*
3. **Bishop Yvette Flunder – Founder of the Fellowship of Affirming Ministries** *"God has always been on the side of the marginalized. As a Black, lesbian bishop, I see the power of God's love working through all people. There is no greater testimony than living your truth and showing that love wins."*

1. **Matthew Vines – Author of 'God and the Gay Christian'** *"The moment I realized that being gay was not a sin, I felt the weight of years of shame lift off me. God's love is not conditional, and no scripture can override the greatest truth: Love is from God, and love is good."*

1. **Reverend Nancy Wilson – Former Moderator of the Metropolitan Community Church** *"When I first felt the call to ministry, I feared that my identity would disqualify me. But I came to realize that my*

queerness was not a barrier to God's love—it was a testament to the diversity of creation."

Finding Peace: Steps Toward Reconciliation

For those who are struggling with faith and identity, here are some steps that can help in the journey of reconciliation:

- **Study the Bible with a Fresh Perspective**

  ○ Read affirming books and theological arguments that challenge traditional interpretations of scripture.

  ○ Seek out passages that emphasize love, inclusion, and the dignity of all people.

- **Connect with LGBTQ+-Affirming Faith Communities**

  ○ Many churches and religious organizations welcome LGBTQ+ members. Look for inclusive denominations such as the Episcopal Church, the United Church of Christ, and the Metropolitan Community Church.

- **Pray and Seek Divine Guidance**

  ○ Approach God with honesty. Ask for clarity, peace, and affirmation. Trust that God's love extends to all, without exception.

- **Embrace Your Identity as God's Creation**

○ Understand that your sexuality and gender identity are not mistakes—they are intentional parts of who you are.

● **Surround Yourself with Support**

○ Find a supportive community of believers who affirm your worth and love you unconditionally.

● **Advocate for Change**

○ If safe to do so, use your voice to advocate for a more inclusive and loving interpretation of faith.

A Final Word of Encouragement

Romans 8:38-39 (KJV): *"For I am persuaded, that neither death, nor life, nor angels, nor principalities, nor powers, nor things present, nor things to come, nor height, nor depth, nor any other creature, shall be able to separate us from the love of God, which is in Christ Jesus our Lord."*

Romans 8:38-39 (NIV): *"For I am convinced that neither death nor life, neither angels nor demons, neither the present nor the future, nor any powers, neither height nor depth, nor anything else in all creation, will be able to separate us from the love of God that is in Christ Jesus our Lord."*

If you have ever felt unworthy of God's love because of your identity, know this: You are loved. You are valued. And you belong.

10

A New Era of Inclusion and Love

The future of faith is one of inclusion. As the world evolves and understanding deepens, more churches and religious communities are recognizing the importance of embracing LGBTQ+ individuals, affirming their worth, and spreading a message of unconditional love—the very essence of Christ's teachings.

The Shift Toward Inclusion

For centuries, institutionalized religion has often been used as a tool to exclude and marginalized LGBTQ+ individuals. However, as biblical scholarship advances and social attitudes shift, many faith communities are reassessing their interpretations of scripture and choosing a more inclusive path. This transformation is fueled by:

- **A Better Understanding of Biblical Context:** Scholars now acknowledge that many biblical passages once thought to condemn same-sex relationships were misinterpreted or taken out of context.

- **The Testimony of LGBTQ+ Christians:** As more openly LGBTQ+ individuals share their faith journeys, they highlight how deeply spirituality and queerness can coexist.

- **The Growing Movement of Affirming Churches:** Denominations such as the Episcopal Church, the United Church of Christ, and the Evangelical Lutheran Church in America openly welcome LGBTQ+ members and clergy.

- **Interfaith Support for LGBTQ+ Rights:** Beyond Christianity, many Jewish, Buddhist, Hindu, and Muslim communities are working toward greater inclusion and love for all individuals.

What Churches Can Do to Embrace LGBTQ+ Individuals

1. **Explicitly State Affirmation**
   Churches must go beyond silent tolerance and actively affirm

LGBTQ+ individuals. This includes clear statements of inclusion on church websites, in sermons, and within leadership structures.

2. **Reevaluate Theology with Love in Mind**
Faith communities must study scripture through the lens of love and inclusion rather than exclusion and condemnation. Many affirming theologians argue that Jesus' message was one of radical love and acceptance.

1. **Welcome LGBTQ+ Leadership**
Allowing LGBTQ+ individuals to serve as clergy, ministers, and church leaders demonstrates that their faith and leadership are just as valuable as anyone else's.

1. **Provide Pastoral Care and Counseling**
Many LGBTQ+ individuals have experienced religious trauma. Churches must offer pastoral care that helps heal rather than harm.

1. **Engage in Advocacy and Social Justice**
Faith communities have historically been at the forefront of social justice movements. Standing for LGBTQ+ rights aligns with Christ's call to love and uplift the marginalized.

Biblical Support for LGBTQ+ Inclusion

At the heart of Christianity is the commandment to love. When churches affirm LGBTQ+ individuals, they are upholding Jesus' teachings:

- **Romans 13:10 (KJV):** "Love worketh no ill to his neighbour: therefore love is the fulfilling of the law."

- **Romans 13:10 (NIV):** "Love does no harm to a neighbor. Therefore love is the fulfillment of the law."

- **1 John 4:7 (KJV):** "Beloved, let us love one another: for love is of God; and every one that loveth is born of God, and knoweth God."

- **1 John 4:7 (NIV):** "Dear friends, let us love one another, for love comes from God. Everyone who loves has been born of God and knows God."

The Power of Personal Testimonies

Many LGBTQ+ Christians have found peace, joy, and purpose within affirming faith communities. Here are just a few stories:

- **Reverend Dr. Megan Rohrer** – The first openly transgender bishop in a major U.S. Christian denomination, Reverend Rohrer has been an outspoken advocate for LGBTQ+ inclusion in the Lutheran church.

- **Reverend Brandan Robertson** – A queer pastor and author, Robertson has dedicated his ministry to teaching inclusive theology and dismantling anti-LGBTQ+ rhetoric in Christianity.

- **Reverend Winnie Varghese** – An Episcopal priest and LGBTQ+ advocate, she has spoken widely about the intersection of faith and social justice.

- **Reverend Troy Perry** – Founder of the Metropolitan Community Church, Perry has helped thousands of LGBTQ+ individuals find a spiritual home.

A Call to Action: Building a Church for All

The future of faith depends on inclusion. By opening their doors and hearts, religious communities can:

- **Heal the wounds of religious exclusion**

- **Bring more people into the faith**

- **Create a world where love is truly unconditional**

In closing, Jesus' message was one of boundless love. The church is strongest when it reflects that love to all, without exception. The time for a new era of inclusion is now.

Conclusion:

Love is Divine

God's love is vast, limitless, and unconditional. This book is a testament to the truth that LGBTQ+ people are not mistakes—they are divine creations, worthy of love, respect, and spiritual fulfillment.

For too long, many have been told that their existence contradicts God's will, that their love is unnatural, and that they must change who they are to be accepted in the eyes of the Divine. But the foundation of faith is love. 1 John 4:8 (KJV) reminds us, "He that loveth not knoweth not God; for God is love." The New International Version (NIV) states it plainly: "Whoever does not love does not know God, because God is love." This love is not conditional, nor is it limited to those who fit into a narrow definition of righteousness imposed by human interpretation. It is expansive, all-encompassing, and freely given to every one of God's creations.

Love as the Core of Scripture

Throughout the Bible, love is described as the greatest of all virtues. Jesus Himself emphasized love above all else. In Matthew 22:37-40 (KJV), He states, "Thou shalt love the Lord thy God with all thy heart, and with all thy soul, and with all thy mind. This is the first and great commandment. And the second is like unto it, Thou shalt love thy neighbour as thyself. On these two commandments hang all the law and the prophets." The NIV echoes this sentiment: "Love the Lord your God with all your heart and with all your soul and with all your mind." This love is not selective; it does not come with caveats or exceptions. It is inclusive and universal.

The Harm of Misinterpretation

For centuries, religious institutions have misinterpreted scripture, using it as a tool for exclusion rather than inclusion. Many passages used to condemn LGBTQ+ individuals have been taken out of historical and linguistic context. Consider the oft-cited Leviticus 18:22 (KJV): "Thou shalt not lie with mankind, as with womankind: it is abomination." The NIV renders it, "Do not have sexual relations with a man as one does with a woman; that is detestable." However, scholars have pointed out that this passage was written within the context of ancient purity laws, which also prohibited wearing mixed fabrics and eating shellfish.

The original Hebrew word translated as "abomination" (to'evah) often referred to practices that were culturally taboo for the Israelites, not moral absolutes for all time.

Similarly, Romans 1:26-27 is often used to condemn same-sex relationships: "For this cause God gave them up unto vile affections: for even their women did change the natural use into that which is against nature: And likewise also the men, leaving the natural use of the woman, burned in their lust one toward another; men with men working that which is unseemly, and receiving in themselves that recompense of their error which was meet" (KJV). The NIV reads: "Because of this, God gave them over to shameful lusts. Even their women exchanged natural sexual relations for unnatural ones. In the same way, the men also abandoned natural relations with women and were inflamed with lust for one another. Men committed shameful acts with other men, and received in themselves the due penalty for their error."

However, a closer reading reveals that Paul was condemning excessive lust and idolatrous practices, not loving, consensual same-sex relationships. The passage discusses individuals who turned away from God and engaged in exploitative behavior, not those who sought committed, loving relationships.

Love in the Life of Jesus

Jesus Himself never condemned same-sex love. Instead, He constantly reached out to those marginalized by society, including lepers, tax collectors, and women accused of adultery. One powerful example is the story of the Roman centurion and his beloved servant in Matthew 8:5-13. In the KJV, Jesus praises the centurion's faith, saying, "Verily I say unto you, I have not found so great faith, no, not in Israel." The NIV similarly states, "Truly I tell you, I have not found anyone in Israel with such great faith." Many biblical scholars believe that the servant referenced in this passage was not merely a household worker, but the centurion's male lover, as it was common in Roman culture for high-ranking men to have same-sex partners. If Jesus had opposed same-sex relationships, He would have condemned the centurion; instead, He healed his beloved.

The Natural Order of Love

Science and history confirm that same-sex love has always been part of human existence. Anthropological studies show that numerous cultures, from Native American Two-Spirit traditions to ancient Greek and African societies, embraced and honored LGBTQ+ individuals. Furthermore, nature itself displays same-sex love. Over 1,500 animal species have been observed engaging in same-sex pairings, including penguins, dolphins, and lions. If same-sex attraction were unnatural, it would not appear so consistently across creation.

The Call for an Inclusive Church

It is time for churches and religious communities to embrace all believers, regardless of sexual orientation or gender identity. The message of Christ was one of radical love and inclusion. Galatians 3:28 (KJV) declares, "There is neither Jew nor Greek, there is neither bond nor free, there is neither male nor female: for ye are all one in Christ Jesus." The NIV states, "There is neither Jew nor Gentile, neither slave nor free, nor is there male and female, for you are all one in Christ Jesus." This passage underscores that human divisions should not define us—our unity in Christ does.

A Message of Hope

For those who have felt rejected by their faith communities, know this: God's love for you has never wavered. You are not a mistake. You are not broken. You are a divine creation, loved fully and completely by the One who formed you. Jeremiah 1:5 (KJV) affirms this: "Before I formed thee in the belly I knew thee; and before thou camest forth out of the womb I sanctified thee." The NIV echoes this truth: "Before I formed you in the womb I knew you, before you were born I set you apart."

This book is more than just an exploration of scripture, history, and science; it is a call to love and acceptance. It is a beacon of hope for every person who has ever questioned whether they can be both queer and loved by God. The answer is simple: Yes, you can. Because God made you. And He loves you. Let this truth settle in your heart, and may it bring you the peace, affirmation, and joy that you have always deserved. Love is divine, and you are a part of that divine love. Amen.

Here are some powerful books written by LGBTQ+ authors that explore Christianity, faith, spirituality, self-love, and the intersection of being LGBTQ+ and religious beliefs:

Books on LGBTQ+ and Christianity/Faith:

1. **"UnClobber: Rethinking Our Misuse of the Bible on Homosexuality"** – Colby Martin

○ A progressive pastor reinterprets scripture and debunks common anti-LGBTQ+ biblical arguments.

2. **"God and the Gay Christian: The Biblical Case in Support of Same-Sex Relationships"** – Matthew Vines

○ A deep dive into biblical texts that have been used against LGBTQ+ people, showing why they do not actually condemn same-sex love.

3. **"Torn: Rescuing the Gospel from the Gays-vs.-Christians Debate"** – Justin Lee

○ A personal memoir of growing up evangelical and gay, and how he reconciled his faith with his identity.

4. **"Shameless: A Sexual Reformation"** – Nadia Bolz-Weber

○ A progressive Christian perspective on sexuality, gender, and how the church has distorted the message of love and grace.

5. **"Walking the Bridgeless Canyon: Repairing the Breach Between the Church and the LGBT Community"** – Kathy Baldock

○ Explores the historical and cultural shifts that led to anti-LGBTQ+ sentiment in the church.

6. **"Transforming: The Bible and the Lives of Transgender Christians"** – Austen Hartke

○ Examines the experiences of transgender Christians and how the Bible supports their identities.

7. **"Outside the Lines: How Embracing Queerness Will Transform Your Faith"** – Mihee Kim-Kort

○ Explores how queerness expands faith beyond restrictive dogma.

8. **"Does Jesus Really Love Me? A Gay Christian's Pilgrimage in Search of God in America"** – Jeff Chu

○ A journalistic exploration of how LGBTQ+ people navigate faith and spirituality in various Christian communities.

9. **"Queer Virtue: What LGBTQ People Know About Life and Love and How It Can Revitalize Christianity"** – Rev. Elizabeth M. Edman

○ Argues that queerness is a spiritual virtue that aligns with Christian principles.

10. **"Coming Out Christian: How Faithful Christians Can Respond to the Church's Persecution of LGBTQ People"** – Luke Timothy Johnson

● A theological defense of LGBTQ+ inclusion in the church.

Books on Spirituality, Self-Love, and Embracing Identity:

1. **"Black, Gay, British, Christian, Queer: The Church and the Famine of Grace"** – Jarel Robinson-Brown

● A reflection on the intersection of race, sexuality, and faith.

1. **"Rainbow Theology: Bridging Race, Sexuality, and Spirit"** –

Patrick S. Cheng

- Explores LGBTQ+ theology from a multicultural perspective.

1. **"Radical Love: An Introduction to Queer Theology"** – Patrick S. Cheng

- A foundational text on queer theology and how it redefines Christian concepts.

1. **"Our Lives Matter: A Womanist Queer Theology"** – Pamela R. Lightsey

- A theological perspective that centers Black LGBTQ+ women in discussions of faith.

1. **"The Book of Queer Prophets: 24 Writers on Sexuality and Religion"** – Edited by Ruth Hunt

- A collection of essays by LGBTQ+ faith leaders and thinkers.

1. **"A Brief Guide to Ministry with LGBTQIA Youth"** – Cody J. Sanders

- A guide for those supporting LGBTQ+ youth in faith-based settings.

1. **"Surprised by God: How I Learned to Stop Worrying and Love Religion"** – Rabbi Danya Ruttenberg

- A queer-friendly perspective on spirituality and faith.

18. What the Bible Really Says about Homosexuality

Daniel A. Helminiak

- A quick conversation guide to what the Bible does and does not say about Homosexuality

1. **The Handbook** - Will Horn

Books on LGBTQ+ History and Love:

20. **"The Deviant's War: The Homosexual vs. The United States of America"** – Eric Cervini

- The story of the first major LGBTQ+ civil rights activist in America.

21. **"Love Wins: The Lovers and Lawyers Who Fought the Landmark Case for Marriage Equality"** – Debbie Cenziper and Jim Obergefell

- A first-hand account of the battle for marriage equality in the U.S.

22. **"Sister Outsider"** – Audre Lorde

- A collection of essays on race, gender, sexuality, and identity.

These books offer a wide range of perspectives on LGBTQ+ identity and faith, helping readers understand the historical, theological, and personal dimensions of being both queer and spiritual.

Finding a place of worship that embraces inclusivity and affirms LGBTQ+ individuals is essential for many seeking both spiritual growth and a welcoming community. Numerous churches and religious organizations across the United States and worldwide are committed to such inclusivity. Below is a curated list of resources and specific congregations that embody these values:

Resources to Locate Inclusive Churches:

1. **Gay Church** – This platform offers an extensive Affirming Church Directory™, allowing users to locate LGBTQ+ affirming Christian congregations globally. The website can be found atwww.gaychurch.org[1].

2. **Church Clarity** – A crowd-sourced database evaluating Christian congregations based on the clarity of their policies regarding LGBTQ+ inclusion and women's roles in leadership. The website can be found atwww.churchclarity.org[2].

3. **Association of Welcoming & Affirming Baptists (AWAB)** – An organization comprising Baptist churches that are open and affirming to LGBTQ+ individuals. The website can be found atwww.awab.org[3].

4. **Reconciling Ministries Network** – Focuses on the inclusion of LGBTQ+ individuals within the United Methodist Church, offering a directory of reconciling ministries. The website can be found atwww.rmnetwork.org[4].

5. **Inclusive Church** – A network of churches in the UK and abroad committed to inclusivity, providing a directory of member churches. The website can be found atwww.inclusive-church.org[5].

1. http://www.gaychurch.org

2. http://www.churchclarity.org

3. http://www.awab.org

4. http://www.rmnetwork.org

5. http://www.inclusive-church.org

Note: While comprehensive directories exist, it's advisable to contact individual churches directly to confirm their current stance on LGBTQ+ inclusion, as policies and leadership can change over time.

These resources and examples demonstrate that inclusive and affirming places of worship are available across the United States and globally, offering spiritual homes where LGBTQ+ individuals can practice their faith openly and authentically.

Examples of LGBTQ+ Affirming Churches in the United States:

- **Metropolitan Community Church of Washington, D.C.**

Address: 474 Ridge St NW, Washington, DC 20001

Religious Leader: Rev. Candy Holmes

Website:www.mccdc.com[6]

- **Covenant Baptist United Church of Christ**

Address: 3845 S Capitol St SW, Washington, DC 20032

Religious Leader: Rev. Dr. Dennis W. Wiley

Website:www.covenantbaptistucc.org[7]

- **Highland Baptist Church**

Address: 1101 Cherokee Rd, Louisville, KY 40204

Website:www.highlandbaptistchurch.org[8]

- **First Baptist Church of Madison**

Address: 518 N Franklin Ave, Madison, WI 53705

---

6. http://www.mccdc.com

7. http://www.covenantbaptistucc.org

8. http://www.highlandbaptistchurch.org

Website:www.firstbaptistmadison.org[9]

• Immanuel Baptist Church

Address: 1101 Lexington Rd, Frankfort, KY 40601

Website:www.immanuelbaptistfrankfort.org[10]

• The Madison Church

Location: Madison, New Hampshire, USA

Website:www.themadisonchurch.org[11]

• Federated Church of Livingston

Location: Livingston, New Jersey, USA

Website:www.federatedchurchlivingston.org[12]

9. http://www.firstbaptistmadison.org

10. http://www.immanuelbaptistfrankfort.org

11. http://www.themadisonchurch.org

12. http://www.federatedchurchlivingston.org

- **First Baptist Church of Moorestown**

Location: Moorestown, New Jersey, USA

Website:www.firstbaptistmoorestown.org[13]

- **Christ Congregation**

Location: Princeton, New Jersey, USA

Website:www.christcongregationprinceton.org[14]

- **Emmanuel Baptist Church**

Location: Ridgewood, New Jersey, USA

Website:www.emmanuelbaptistridgewood.org[15]

---

13. http://www.firstbaptistmoorestown.org

14. http://www.christcongregationprinceton.org

15. http://www.emmanuelbaptistridgewood.org

Notes

Notes

Notes

Notes

www.ingramcontent.com/pod-product-compliance
Lightning Source LLC
La Vergne TN
LVHW021402080426
835508LV00020B/2418